Alaskan Eskimos and Aleuts

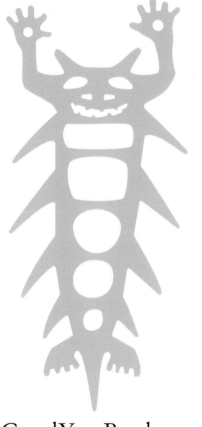

By Mira Bartók and
Christine Ronan

GoodYearBooks

An Imprint of ScottForesman
A Division of HarperCollinsPublishers

Alaska

Canada

United States

This book is about the Eskimo and Aleut peoples who live in Alaska and the surrounding islands.

On the coast and arctic tundra
where they live, there are many
forms of wildlife.

Arctic peoples hunt seals, whales,
and walruses for blubber. Blubber
is used for food and oil.

People use other parts of sea
mammals to make objects such as
drums.

See how high you can bounce on a
walrus skin blanket!

Some people
thank the
animals that feed
and clothe them
by painting
pictures of their
spirits or *inuas*.

10

The picture above shows a caribou (red) connected to its inua (blue).

They thank the animals by
drumming and dancing too!

Children keep their culture alive
by learning the ancient ways from
their elders.